HEALTHY
RECIPES

FOR THE HOLIDAYS

Front cover and contents page photography: Sacco Productions Limited, Chicago
All other photography: Audrey Nilsen Photography, Chicago

Pictured on the front cover: Roast Turkey with Cranberry Stuffing *(page 42)* and Spicy Southwestern Vegetable Sauté *(page 66)*.

Pictured on the back cover *(from top to bottom):* Mustard-Crusted Roast Pork *(page 52)*, Smoked Salmon Appetizers *(page 14)*, Spicy Pumpkin Soup with Green Chili Swirl *(page 26)* and Turtle Cheesecake *(page 88)*.

ISBN: 0-7853-6135-9

Manufactured in China.

8 7 6 5 4 3 2 1

Microwave Cooking: Microwave ovens vary in wattage. Use the cooking times as guidelines and check for doneness before adding more time.

CONTENTS

LESSONS IN SMART EATING

Today, people everywhere are more aware than ever before about the importance of maintaining a healthful lifestyle. In addition to proper exercise, this includes eating foods that are lower in fat, sodium and cholesterol. The goal of this magazine is to provide today's cook with easy-to-prepare recipes that taste great, yet easily fit into today's dietary goals. Eating well is a matter of making smarter choices about the foods you eat. Preparing these recipes is your first step toward making smart choices a delicious reality.

Lower Fat for Healthier Living

It is widely known that most Americans' diets are too high in fat. A low-fat diet reduces your risk of getting certain diseases and helps you maintain a healthy weight. Studies have shown that eating more than the recommended amount of fat (especially saturated fat) is associated with increased blood cholesterol levels in some adults. A high blood cholesterol level is associated with increased risk for heart disease. A high-fat diet may also increase your chances for obesity and some types of cancer.

Nutrition experts recommend diets that contain 30% or less of total daily calories from fat. The "30% calories from fat" goal applies to a total diet over time, not to a single food, serving of a recipe or meal. To find the approximate percentage of calories from fat use this easy 3-step process:

1 Multiply the grams of fat per serving by 9 (there are 9 calories in each gram of fat), to give you the number of calories from fat per serving.

2 Divide by the total number of calories per serving.

3 Multiply by 100%.

For example, imagine a 200-calorie sandwich that has 10 grams of fat.

To find the percentage of calories from fat, first multiply the grams of
fat by 9:

$$10 \times 9 = 90$$

Then, divide by the total number of calories in a serving:

$$90 \div 200 = .45$$

Multiply by 100% to get the percentage of calories from fat:

$$.45 \times 100\% = 45\%$$

You may find doing all this math tiresome, so an easier way to keep track of the fat in your diet is to calculate the total *grams* of fat appropriate to your caloric intake, then keep a running count of fat grams over the course of a day.

Defining "Fat Free"

It is important to take the time to read food labels carefully. For example, you'll find many food products on the grocery store shelves making claims such as "97% fat free." This does not necessarily mean that 97% of the *calories* are free from fat (or that only 3 percent of calories come from fat). Often these numbers are calculated by weight. This means that out of 100 grams of this food, 3 grams are fat. Depending on what else is in the food, the percentage of calories from fat can be quite high. You may find that the percent of calories *from fat* can be as high as 50%.

Daily Values

Fat has become the focus of many diets and eating plans. This is because most Americans' diets are too high in fat. However, there are other important nutrients to be aware of, including saturated fat, sodium, cholesterol, protein, carbohydrates and several vitamins and minerals. Daily values for these nutrients have been established by the government and reflect current nutritional recommendations for a 2,000-calorie reference diet. They are appropriate for most adults and children (age 4 or older) and provide excellent guidelines for an overall healthy diet.

Nutritional Analysis

Every recipe in this magazine is followed by a nutritional analysis block that lists certain nutrient values for a single serving.

■ The analysis of each recipe includes all the ingredients that are listed in that recipe, *except* ingredients labeled as "optional" or "for garnish." Nutritional analysis is provided for the primary recipe only, not for the recipe variations.

■ If a range is offered for an ingredient ("¼ to ⅛ teaspoon" for example), the *first* amount given was used to calculate the nutrition information.

■ If an ingredient is presented with an option ("2 cups hot cooked rice or noodles" for example), the *first* item listed was used to calculate the nutritional information.

■ Foods shown in photographs on the same serving plate and offered as "serve with" suggestions at the end of a recipe are *not* included in the recipe analysis unless they are listed in the ingredient list.

■ In recipes calling for cooked rice or noodles, the analysis was based on rice or noodles that were prepared without added salt or fat unless otherwise mentioned in the recipe.

The nutrition information that appears with each recipe was calculated by an independent nutrition consulting firm. Every effort has been made to check the accuracy of these numbers. However, because numerous variables account for a wide range of values in certain foods, all analyses that appear in this magazine should be considered approximate.

The recipes in this publication are *not* intended as a medically therapeutic program, nor as a substitute for medically approved diet plans for people on fat, cholesterol or sodium restricted diets. You should consult your physician before beginning any diet plan. The recipes offered here can be a part of a healthy lifestyle that meets recognized dietary guidelines. A healthy lifestyle includes not only eating a balanced diet, but engaging in proper exercise as well.

Cooking Healthier

When preparing these low-fat recipes, you will find some techniques or ingredients are different from traditional cooking. Fat serves as a flavor enhancer and gives foods a distinctive and desirable texture. In order to compensate for the lack of fat and still give great-tasting results, many of these recipes call for a selection of herbs or a combination of fresh vegetables. A wide variety of grains and pastas are also used. Many of the recipes call for alternative protein sources, such as dried beans or tofu. Often meat is included in a recipe as an accent flavor rather than the star attraction. Vegetables are often "sautéed" in a small amount of broth rather than oil. Applesauce may be added to baked goods to give a texture similar to full fat foods. These are all simple changes that you can easily make when you start cooking healthy! Following are some general guidelines on cutting the fat and calories in your own family's favorite meals.

Cutting the Fat

■ Limit red meat, including beef, lamb and pork to three servings a week. Eat no more than four ounces per meal.

■ Eat more seafood and skinless poultry, but keep portions to three to four ounces.

■ Eat a meatless dinner once or twice a week.

■ Try cutting fat by half during preparation and at the table. For example, use less oil in a stir-fry dish or try a nonstick cooking spray to grease your pan instead of butter. Use less salad dressing, or substitute a low-fat version.

■ Switch to low-fat products. Look for nonfat or low-fat mayonnaise and sour cream to reduce your fat intake.

■ Eat at least five servings of fruit and vegetables daily. You'll feel more satisfied and have less room for high-fat snack foods, such as chips and cookies.

■ Study food labels. Use foods high in saturated fat sparingly.

■ Try switching to reduced-fat cheese and low-fat cottage cheese.

■ Trim the fat from meat and the skin from chicken before cooking, so the seasoning can go directly into the meat rather than the fat and skin.

APPETIZERS & DRINKS

SPICY VEGETABLE QUESADILLAS

These Southwestern treats are the perfect starters for any party or family gathering. Full of flavor and spice, no one will suspect they're so low in fat.

Nonstick cooking spray
1 small zucchini, chopped
½ cup chopped green bell
   pepper
½ cup chopped onion
2 cloves garlic, minced

½ teaspoon ground cumin
½ teaspoon chili powder
8 (6-inch) flour tortillas
1 cup (4 ounces) shredded
   reduced-fat Cheddar cheese
¼ cup chopped fresh cilantro

1 Spray large nonstick skillet with cooking spray. Heat over medium heat until hot. Add zucchini, pepper, onion, garlic, cumin and chili powder; cook and stir 3 to 4 minutes or until vegetables are crisp-tender. Remove vegetable mixture and set aside; wipe skillet clean.

2 Spoon vegetable mixture evenly over half of each tortilla. Sprinkle each evenly with cheese and cilantro. Fold each tortilla in half.

3 Spray same skillet with cooking spray. Add tortillas and heat 1 to 2 minutes per side over medium heat or until lightly browned. Cut into thirds before serving.

Makes 8 servings

Nutrients per Serving:

Calories	153 (22% calories from fat)					
Total Fat	4 g	Carbohydrate	23 g	Iron		trace
Saturated Fat	1 g	Dietary Fiber	1 g	Vitamin A		56 RE
Cholesterol	8 mg	Protein	7 g	Vitamin C		15 mg
Sodium	201 mg	Calcium	112 mg	Sugar		1 g

DIETARY EXCHANGES: 1½ Starch/Bread, ½ Lean Meat, ½ Fat

PINEAPPLE GINGER SHRIMP COCKTAIL

Combining the tropical treasures of pineapple and ginger with America's favorite shellfish results in a delectable taste sensation. Cooked, shelled shrimp should look succulent and plump with no hint of ammonia odor. Fresh pineapple spears are available in the produce section of most supermarkets.

9 fresh pineapple spears (about 1 package), divided
¼ cup all-fruit apricot preserves
1 tablespoon finely chopped onion
½ teaspoon grated fresh ginger

⅛ teaspoon ground black pepper
8 ounces cooked medium shrimp (about 30)
1 red or green bell pepper, cut into 12 strips

1 Chop 3 pineapple spears into bite-sized pieces; combine with preserves, onion, ginger and black pepper in medium bowl.

2 Evenly arrange shrimp, bell pepper strips and remaining pineapple spears on 6 small plates lined with lettuce leaves, if desired. Add one spoonful of pineapple mixture to each plate.   *Makes 6 servings*

Nutrients per Serving:

Calories	108 (6% calories from fat)				
Total Fat	1 g	Carbohydrate	20 g	Iron	2 mg
Saturated Fat	trace	Dietary Fiber	2 g	Vitamin A	264 RE
Cholesterol	58 mg	Protein	7 g	Vitamin C	95 mg
Sodium	69 mg	Calcium	24 mg	Sugar	7 g

DIETARY EXCHANGES: 1 Lean Meat, ½ Fruit, 1 Vegetable

SMOKED SALMON APPETIZERS

Turn the classic combination of lox, bagels and cream cheese into an elegant opening for your holiday festivities. Lox is smoked salmon that has been brine-cured before smoking, resulting in a saltier taste; if you wish, ask for the less salty "Nova" lox.

¼ cup reduced-fat or fat-free cream cheese, softened
1 tablespoon chopped fresh dill *or* 1 teaspoon dried dill weed

⅛ teaspoon ground red pepper
4 ounces thinly sliced smoked salmon or lox
24 melba toast rounds or other low-fat crackers

1 Combine cream cheese, dill and pepper in small bowl; stir to blend. Spread evenly over each slice of salmon. Starting with short side, roll up salmon slices jelly-roll fashion. Place on plate; cover with plastic wrap. Chill at least 1 hour or up to 4 hours before serving.

2 Using a sharp knife, cut salmon rolls crosswise into ¾-inch pieces. Place pieces, cut side down, on serving plate. Garnish each piece with dill sprig, if desired. Serve cold or at room temperature with melba rounds.

Makes about 2 dozen appetizers (3 appetizers per serving)

Nutrients per Serving:

Calories	80 (21% calories from fat)				
Total Fat	2 g	Carbohydrate	10 g	Iron	trace
Saturated Fat	1 g	Dietary Fiber	1 g	Vitamin A	36 RE
Cholesterol	6 mg	Protein	6 g	Vitamin C	trace
Sodium	241 mg	Calcium	27 mg	Sugar	0 g

DIETARY EXCHANGES: ½ Starch/Bread, ½ Lean Meat

SOUTHERN CRAB CAKES WITH RÉMOULADE DIPPING SAUCE

10 ounces fresh lump crabmeat
1½ cups fresh white or sourdough bread crumbs, divided
¼ cup chopped green onions
½ cup nonfat or reduced-fat mayonnaise, divided
2 tablespoons coarse grain or spicy brown mustard, divided
¾ teaspoon hot pepper sauce, divided
1 egg white, lightly beaten
2 teaspoons olive oil, divided
Lemon wedges

1 Preheat oven to 200°F. Combine crabmeat, ¾ cup bread crumbs and green onions in medium bowl. Add ¼ cup mayonnaise, 1 tablespoon mustard, ½ teaspoon pepper sauce and egg white; mix well. Using ¼ cup mixture per cake, shape eight ½-inch-thick cakes. Roll crab cakes lightly in remaining ¾ cup bread crumbs.

2 Heat large nonstick skillet over medium heat until hot; add 1 teaspoon oil. Add 4 crab cakes; cook 4 to 5 minutes per side or until golden brown. Transfer to serving platter; keep warm in oven. Repeat with remaining 1 teaspoon oil and crab cakes.

3 To prepare dipping sauce, combine remaining ¼ cup mayonnaise, 1 tablespoon mustard and ¼ teaspoon pepper sauce in small bowl; mix well.

4 Serve warm crab cakes with lemon wedges and dipping sauce.

Makes 8 servings

Nutrients per Serving:

Calories	81 (25% calories from fat)				
Total Fat	2 g	Carbohydrate	8 g	Iron	1 mg
Saturated Fat	trace	Dietary Fiber	trace	Vitamin A	13 RE
Cholesterol	30 mg	Protein	7 g	Vitamin C	1 mg
Sodium	376 mg	Calcium	48 mg	Sugar	trace

DIETARY EXCHANGES: ½ Starch/Bread, 1 Lean Meat

SHRIMP DIP WITH CRUDITÉS

Any combination of raw vegetables, including broccoli, cauliflower or celery, can be added to this simple, yet elegant appetizer. Be sure to choose veggies of different colors and shapes to create an eye-catching display.

1 can (6 ounces) cooked
    shrimp, drained, divided
½ cup reduced-fat cream
    cheese, softened
⅓ cup plus 1 tablespoon thinly
    sliced green onions, divided
3 tablespoons light or fat-free
    Caesar salad dressing
2 teaspoons prepared
    horseradish

¼ teaspoon salt
2 red or yellow bell peppers,
    cut into 2×1-inch pieces
4 large carrots, peeled,
    diagonally sliced ¼ inch
    thick
10 crispbread or other low-fat
    crackers

1 Reserve several shrimp for garnish. Combine remaining shrimp, cream cheese, ⅓ cup green onions, salad dressing, horseradish and salt in medium bowl; mix well. Transfer to serving dish; top with reserved shrimp and remaining 1 tablespoon green onions. Cover and chill at least 30 minutes before serving.

2 Serve with bell peppers, carrots and crackers.   *Makes 10 servings*

Nutrients per Serving:

Calories	127 (29% calories from fat)				
Total Fat	4 g	Carbohydrate	16 g	Iron	1 mg
Saturated Fat	trace	Dietary Fiber	2 g	Vitamin A	1133 RE
Cholesterol	37 mg	Protein	7 g	Vitamin C	106 mg
Sodium	217 mg	Calcium	41 mg	Sugar	2 g

DIETARY EXCHANGES: ½ Starch/Bread, ½ Lean Meat, 2 Vegetable, ½ Fat

CRANBERRY-LIME MARGARITA PUNCH

This refreshing and festive punch adds sparkle and panache to any occasion.

6 cups water
1 container (12 ounces) frozen
    cranberry juice cocktail
½ cup lime juice

¼ cup sugar
2 cups ice cubes
1 cup ginger ale or tequila
1 lime, sliced

 Combine water, cranberry juice, lime juice and sugar in punch bowl; stir until sugar dissolves.

 Stir in ice cubes, ginger ale and lime; garnish with fresh cranberries, if desired.

Makes 10 servings

Nutrients per Serving:

Calories	97 (0% calories from fat)				
Total Fat	trace	Carbohydrate	25 g	Iron	trace
Saturated Fat	trace	Dietary Fiber	trace	Vitamin A	1 RE
Cholesterol	0 mg	Protein	trace	Vitamin C	32 mg
Sodium	3 mg	Calcium	8 mg	Sugar	7 g

DIETARY EXCHANGES: 1½ Fruit

❖

Cook's Tip

Add a festive touch to your holidays by adding a colorful and appealing ice ring to your punch bowl. Simply fill a ring mold with some punch and fresh cranberries, freeze until solid, unmold and float the ice ring in the punch bowl.

❖

OREGON HOT APPLE CIDER

To warm up those cold holiday nights, sit by the fire and sip this enticing classic direct from the Pacific Northwest. The pear provides an elegant touch.

8 whole cloves
8 cups apple cider
½ cup dried cherries
½ cup dried cranberries

3 cinnamon sticks, broken in
  half
1 pear, quartered, cored, sliced

 Bundle cloves in small piece of cheesecloth. Tie cheesecloth to form small sack.

 Combine cider, cherries, cranberries, cinnamon and cheesecloth sack in large saucepan. Heat just to a simmer; do not boil. Remove cheesecloth sack and discard.

 Add pear before serving. *Makes 8 servings*

Nutrients per Serving:

Calories	180 (3% calories from fat)				
Total Fat	1 g	Carbohydrate	48 g	Iron	2 mg
Saturated Fat	trace	Dietary Fiber	2 g	Vitamin A	97 RE
Cholesterol	0 mg	Protein	1 g	Vitamin C	13 mg
Sodium	10 mg	Calcium	31 mg	Sugar	2 g

DIETARY EXCHANGES: 3 Fruit

❖

Cook's Tip
To quickly ripen a pear, place it, along with an apple,
in a paper bag. Poke a few holes in the bag with a
knife and let the bag stand at room temperature.

❖

SALADS & SOUPS

PEAR AND CRANBERRY SALAD

Bring a touch of elegance to the holidays and create a medley of robust flavors. Be sure to use ripe pears; Forelles and Red Bartletts are particularly well suited for use in this salad. A high-quality balsamic vinegar is a wonderful addition to your pantry.

½ cup canned whole berry
    cranberry sauce
2 tablespoons balsamic vinegar
1 tablespoon olive or canola oil
12 cups (9 ounces) packed
    assorted bitter or gourmet
    salad greens

6 small or 4 large pears (about
    1¾ pounds)
2 ounces blue or Gorgonzola
    cheese, crumbled
Freshly ground black pepper

1 Combine cranberry sauce, vinegar and oil in small bowl; mix well. (Dressing may be covered and refrigerated up to 2 days before serving.)

2 Arrange greens on six serving plates. Cut pears lengthwise into ½-inch-thick slices; cut core and seeds from each slice. Arrange pears attractively over greens. Drizzle cranberry dressing over pears and greens; sprinkle with cheese. Sprinkle with pepper to taste.

Makes 6 servings

Nutrients per Serving:

Calories	161 (29% calories from fat)				
Total Fat	6 g	Carbohydrate	26 g	Iron	1 mg
Saturated Fat	2 g	Dietary Fiber	2 g	Vitamin A	313 RE
Cholesterol	7 mg	Protein	4 g	Vitamin C	20 mg
Sodium	165 mg	Calcium	122 mg	Sugar	1 g

DIETARY EXCHANGES: 2 Fruit, 1 Fat

SPICY PUMPKIN SOUP WITH GREEN CHILI SWIRL

Warm up the winter holidays with this Southwestern special featuring regional spices and the added kick of green chilies. Chilies may be rinsed in cold water before using to decrease spiciness.

1 can (4 ounces) diced green chilies, drained
¼ cup reduced-fat sour cream
¼ cup fresh cilantro leaves
1 can (15 ounces) solid-pack pumpkin
1 can (about 14 ounces) fat-free reduced-sodium chicken broth

½ cup water
1 teaspoon ground cumin
½ teaspoon chili powder
¼ teaspoon garlic powder
⅛ teaspoon ground red pepper (optional)

1 Combine green chilies, sour cream and cilantro in food processor or blender; process until smooth.*

2 Combine pumpkin, chicken broth, water, cumin, chili powder, garlic powder and pepper, if desired, in medium saucepan; stir in ¼ cup green chili mixture. Bring to a boil; reduce heat to medium. Simmer, uncovered, 5 minutes, stirring occasionally.

3 Pour into serving bowls. Top each serving with small dollops of remaining green chili mixture and additional sour cream, if desired. Run tip of spoon through dollops to swirl.   *Makes 4 servings*

*Omit food processor step by adding green chilies directly to soup. Finely chop cilantro and combine with sour cream. Dollop with sour cream mixture as directed.

Nutrients per Serving:

Calories	72 (17% calories from fat)					
Total Fat	1 g	Carbohydrate	12 g	Iron	2 mg
Saturated Fat	trace	Dietary Fiber	4 g	Vitamin A	2424 RE
Cholesterol	5 mg	Protein	4 g	Vitamin C	5 mg
Sodium	276 mg	Calcium	57 mg	Sugar	0 g

DIETARY EXCHANGES: 1 Starch/Bread

CRAB COBB SALAD

Fresh or pasteurized crabmeat can be substituted for the canned variety. Crabmeat should always smell fresh and sweet; lump and backfin meat are the best kinds.

12 cups washed and torn
   romaine lettuce
2 cans (6 ounces each)
   crabmeat, drained
2 cups diced ripe tomatoes or
   halved cherry tomatoes
¼ cup (1½ ounces) crumbled
   blue or Gorgonzola cheese

¼ cup cholesterol-free bacon
   bits
¾ cup fat-free Italian or Caesar
   salad dressing
Freshly ground black pepper

 Cover large serving platter with lettuce. Arrange crabmeat, tomatoes, blue cheese and bacon bits attractively over lettuce.

 Just before serving, drizzle dressing evenly over salad; toss well. Transfer to 8 chilled serving plates; sprinkle with pepper to taste.

Makes 8 servings

Nutrients per Serving:

Calories	110 (27% calories from fat)					
Total Fat	3 g	Carbohydrate	8 g	Iron	2 mg
Saturated Fat	1 g	Dietary Fiber	2 g	Vitamin A	262 RE
Cholesterol	46 mg	Protein	12 g	Vitamin C	31 mg
Sodium	666 mg	Calcium	75 mg	Sugar	3 g

DIETARY EXCHANGES: 1½ Lean Meat, 1½ Vegetable

❖

Cook's Tip

This salad can be covered and refrigerated up to five hours before serving. Toss with dressing immediately before serving.

❖

TEXAS-STYLE CHILI

Called a "bowl of red" deep in the heart of Texas, this chili is usually served with the beans on the side. For those who like their chili with a bit more fire, use a hotter salsa or even a few dashes of hot pepper sauce. This dish is even better when it's prepared a day ahead, chilled and brought back to a simmer before serving.

Nonstick cooking spray
1 pound lean boneless beef chuck, cut into ½-inch pieces
2 cups chopped onions
5 cloves garlic, minced
2 tablespoons chili powder
1 tablespoon ground cumin
1 teaspoon ground coriander
1 teaspoon dried oregano leaves or ground oregano

2½ cups fat-free reduced-sodium beef broth
1 cup prepared salsa or picante sauce
2 cans (16 ounces each) pinto or red beans (or one of each), rinsed and drained
½ cup chopped fresh cilantro
½ cup nonfat sour cream
1 cup chopped ripe tomatoes

1 Spray Dutch oven or large saucepan with nonstick cooking spray; heat over medium-high heat until hot. Add beef, onions and garlic; cook and stir until beef is no longer pink, about 5 minutes. Sprinkle mixture with chili powder, cumin, coriander and oregano; mix well. Add beef broth and salsa; bring to a boil. Cover; simmer 45 minutes.

2 Stir in beans; continue to simmer uncovered 30 minutes or until beef is tender and chili has thickened, stirring occasionally.

3 Stir in cilantro. Ladle into bowls; top with sour cream and tomatoes. Garnish with pickled jalapeño peppers, if desired.　　*Makes 8 servings*

Nutrients per Serving:

Calories	268 (21% calories from fat)				
Total Fat	7 g	Carbohydrate	31 g	Iron	3 mg
Saturated Fat	2 g	Dietary Fiber	2 g	Vitamin A	194 RE
Cholesterol	37 mg	Protein	25 g	Vitamin C	21 mg
Sodium	725 mg	Calcium	62 mg	Sugar	2 g

DIETARY EXCHANGES: 1½ Starch/Bread, 2½ Lean Meat, 1 Vegetable

DOUBLE CORN & CHEDDAR CHOWDER

You'll swear you're in the heartland of the Midwest when you indulge in this soup—it's so rich and creamy your family and friends won't believe it's low in fat and cholesterol. Replace some of the chicken broth with light beer to produce a truly authentic Wisconsin specialty.

1 tablespoon margarine
1 cup chopped onion
2 tablespoons all-purpose flour
2½ cups fat-free reduced-sodium chicken broth
1 can (16 ounces) cream-style corn
1 cup frozen whole kernel corn

½ cup finely diced red bell pepper
½ teaspoon hot pepper sauce
¾ cup (3 ounces) shredded sharp Cheddar cheese
Freshly ground black pepper (optional)

1 Melt margarine in large saucepan over medium heat. Add onion; cook and stir 5 minutes. Sprinkle onion with flour; cook and stir 1 minute.

2 Add chicken broth; bring to a boil, stirring frequently. Add cream-style corn, corn kernels, bell pepper and pepper sauce; bring to a simmer. Cover; simmer 15 minutes.

3 Remove from heat; gradually stir in cheese until melted. Ladle into soup bowls; sprinkle with black pepper, if desired.   *Makes 6 servings*

Double Corn, Cheddar & Rice Chowder: Add 1 cup cooked white or brown rice with corn.

Nutrients per Serving:

Calories	180 (28% calories from fat)				
Total Fat	6 g	Carbohydrate	28 g	Iron	1 mg
Saturated Fat	2 g	Dietary Fiber	2 g	Vitamin A	177 RE
Cholesterol	10 mg	Protein	7 g	Vitamin C	49 mg
Sodium	498 mg	Calcium	88 mg	Sugar	1 g

DIETARY EXCHANGES: 1½ Starch/Bread, ½ Lean Meat, 1 Fat

SANTA FE GRILLED VEGETABLE SALAD

Nothing beats the flavor of food off the grill, especially if the marinade is as robust as this citrus-enhanced Southwestern fare. You may want to peel the eggplant after grilling, as the skin may be slightly bitter.

1 medium yellow summer squash, cut into halves

1 medium zucchini, cut into halves

1 green bell pepper, cut into quarters

1 red bell pepper, cut into quarters

2 baby eggplants (6 ounces each), cut into halves

1 small onion, peeled, cut into halves

½ cup orange juice

2 tablespoons lime juice

1 tablespoon olive oil

2 cloves garlic, minced

1 teaspoon dried oregano leaves

¼ teaspoon salt

¼ teaspoon ground red pepper

¼ teaspoon ground black pepper

2 tablespoons chopped fresh cilantro

1 Combine all ingredients except cilantro in large bowl; toss to coat.

2 To prevent sticking, spray grid with nonstick cooking spray. Prepare coals for grilling. Place vegetables on grid, 2 to 3 inches from hot coals; reserve marinade. Grill 3 to 4 minutes per side or until tender and lightly charred; cool 10 minutes. Or, place vegetables on rack of broiler pan coated with nonstick cooking spray; reserve marinade. Broil 2 to 3 inches from heat, 3 to 4 minutes per side or until tender; cool 10 minutes.

3 Remove peel from eggplants, if desired. Slice vegetables into bite-sized pieces; return to reserved marinade. Stir in cilantro; toss to coat.

Makes 8 servings

Nutrients per Serving:

Calories	63 (27% calories from fat)					
Total Fat	2 g	Carbohydrate	11 g	Iron	1 mg
Saturated Fat	trace	Dietary Fiber	1 g	Vitamin A	210 RE
Cholesterol	0 mg	Protein	2 g	Vitamin C	85 mg
Sodium	70 mg	Calcium	27 mg	Sugar	2 g

DIETARY EXCHANGES: 2 Vegetable, ½ Fat

SPINACH SALAD WITH HOT APPLE DRESSING

Even though green leafy vegetables, like spinach, are some of the healthiest foods you can eat, it used to be difficult to make them appealing and tempting—until now! Turkey bacon offers all the flavor of regular bacon with nearly half the saturated fat.

6 strips turkey bacon
¾ cup apple cider
2 tablespoons brown sugar
4 teaspoons rice wine vinegar
¼ teaspoon ground black pepper
6 cups washed and torn spinach
    leaves

2 cups sliced mushrooms
1 medium tomato, cut into
    wedges
½ cup thinly sliced red onion

1 Heat medium nonstick skillet over medium heat until hot; add bacon and cook 2 to 3 minutes per side or until crisp; remove from pan. Coarsely chop 3 pieces; set aside. Finely chop remaining 3 pieces; return to skillet. Add apple cider, sugar, vinegar and pepper. Heat just to a simmer; remove from heat.

2 Combine spinach, mushrooms, tomato and onion in large bowl. Add dressing; toss to coat. Top with reserved bacon.   *Makes 6 servings*

Nutrients per Serving:

Calories	95 (28% calories from fat)				
Total Fat	3 g	Carbohydrate	14 g	Iron	2 mg
Saturated Fat	1 g	Dietary Fiber	2 g	Vitamin A	389 RE
Cholesterol	9 mg	Protein	5 g	Vitamin C	22 mg
Sodium	256 mg	Calcium	74 mg	Sugar	1 g

DIETARY EXCHANGES: ½ Fruit, 1½ Vegetable, ½ Fat

NEW ENGLAND CLAM CHOWDER

The word "chowder" comes from the French word chaudière, *the stew pot in which fishermen cooked their catches of the day. The New England version features milk, while the Manhattan (or red) variety adds tomatoes to the basic recipe.*

1 can (5 ounces) whole baby
   clams, undrained
1 baking potato, peeled,
   coarsely chopped
¼ cup finely chopped onion

⅔ cup evaporated skimmed milk
¼ teaspoon ground white pepper
¼ teaspoon dried thyme leaves
1 tablespoon reduced-calorie
   margarine

1 Drain clams; reserve juice. Add enough water to reserved juice to measure ⅔ cup. Combine clam juice mixture, potato and onion in medium saucepan. Bring to a boil over high heat; reduce heat and simmer 8 minutes or until potato is tender.

2 Add milk, pepper and thyme to saucepan. Increase heat to medium-high. Cook and stir 2 minutes. Add margarine. Cook 5 minutes or until chowder thickens, stirring occasionally.

3 Add clams; cook and stir 5 minutes or until clams are firm.

Makes 2 servings

Nutrients per Serving:

Calories	191 (18% calories from fat)				
Total Fat	4 g	Carbohydrate	27 g	Iron	4 mg
Saturated Fat	1 g	Dietary Fiber	1 g	Vitamin A	164 RE
Cholesterol	47 mg	Protein	14 g	Vitamin C	7 mg
Sodium	205 mg	Calcium	298 mg	Sugar	2 g

DIETARY EXCHANGES: 1 Starch/Bread, 1 Lean Meat, 1 Milk

MAIN DISHES

TURKEY & PASTA WITH CILANTRO PESTO

A member of the parsley family, cilantro (also known as coriander leaves) is the world's most widely used herb. Its vibrant flavor infuses this pasta and turkey combination with a Southwestern sensation. Turkey breast cut into strips may be substituted for turkey tenders.

1 pound turkey tenders, cut into strips
3 cloves garlic, minced
½ teaspoon ground cumin
¼ teaspoon ground red pepper
¼ teaspoon ground black pepper
2 tablespoons olive oil
1½ cups chopped seeded tomatoes

½ cup chopped fresh cilantro
¼ cup (1 ounce) grated Parmesan cheese
2 tablespoons orange juice
12 ounces dry linguine, cooked and kept warm

1 Combine turkey, garlic, cumin, red pepper and black pepper in medium bowl; toss to coat. Heat oil in large skillet over medium-high heat. Add turkey mixture; cook 4 to 6 minutes or until turkey is no longer pink in center.

2 Add tomatoes; cook 2 minutes. Stir in cilantro, cheese and orange juice; cook 1 minute.

3 Toss turkey mixture and linguine in large bowl. Serve immediately.

Makes 6 servings

Nutrients per Serving:

Calories	365 (22% calories from fat)					
Total Fat	9 g	Carbohydrate	48 g	Iron	3 mg
Saturated Fat	2 g	Dietary Fiber	1 g	Vitamin A	62 RE
Cholesterol	33 mg	Protein	23 g	Vitamin C	14 mg
Sodium	112 mg	Calcium	91 mg	Sugar	2 g

DIETARY EXCHANGES: 3 Starch/Bread, 1½ Lean Meat, 1 Vegetable, 1 Fat

ROAST TURKEY WITH CRANBERRY STUFFING

A New England twist enlivens this quintessential holiday dish. Taking off the turkey skin eliminates loads of fat without removing any of the succulence.

Cranberry Stuffing (page 44)   1 turkey (8 to 10 pounds)

1 Prepare Cranberry Stuffing. *Reduce oven temperature to 350°F.*

2 Remove giblets from turkey. Rinse turkey and cavity in cold water; pat dry with paper towels. Fill turkey cavity loosely with stuffing. Place remaining stuffing in casserole sprayed with nonstick cooking spray. Cover casserole; refrigerate until baking time.

3 Spray roasting pan with nonstick cooking spray. Place turkey, breast side up, on rack in roasting pan. Bake 3 hours or until thermometer inserted in thickest part of thigh registers 185°F and juices run clear.

4 Transfer turkey to serving platter. Cover loosely with foil; let stand 20 minutes. Place covered casserole of stuffing in oven; *increase oven temperature to 375°F.* Bake 25 to 30 minutes or until hot.

5 Remove and discard turkey skin. Slice turkey and serve with Cranberry Stuffing and Spicy Southwestern Vegetable Sauté (page 66), if desired. Garnish with fresh rosemary sprigs, if desired.

Makes 10 servings

continued on page 44

Roast Turkey with Cranberry Stuffing, continued

CRANBERRY STUFFING

1 loaf (12 ounces) Italian or
French bread, cut into
½-inch cubes
2 tablespoons margarine
1½ cups chopped onions
1½ cups chopped celery
2 teaspoons poultry seasoning
1 teaspoon dried thyme leaves

½ teaspoon dried rosemary
¼ teaspoon salt
¼ teaspoon ground black pepper
1 cup coarsely chopped fresh
cranberries
1 tablespoon sugar
¾ cup fat-free reduced-sodium
chicken broth

1 Preheat oven to 375°F. Arrange bread on two 15×10-inch jelly-roll pans. Bake 12 minutes or until lightly toasted.

2 Melt margarine in large saucepan over medium heat. Add onions and celery. Cook and stir 8 minutes or until vegetables are tender; remove from heat. Add bread cubes, poultry seasoning, thyme, rosemary, salt and pepper; mix well. Combine cranberries and sugar in small bowl; mix well. Add to bread mixture; toss well. Drizzle chicken broth evenly over mixture; toss well. *Makes 10 servings*

Nutrients per Serving:

(turkey and stuffing)

Calories	439 (26% calories from fat)					
Total Fat	12 g	Carbohydrate	23 g	Iron	5 mg
Saturated Fat	4 g	Dietary Fiber	1 g	Vitamin A	32 RE
Cholesterol	136 mg	Protein	56 g	Vitamin C	4 mg
Sodium	445 mg	Calcium	91 mg	Sugar	2 g

DIETARY EXCHANGES: 1½ Starch/Bread, 6 Lean Meat

OVEN-ROASTED BOSTON SCROD

Scrod, another name for young cod, was introduced at the Parker House Hotel in Boston in the 1890's. Scrod's naturally delicate flavor and flaky texture dominate this easy-to-prepare dish.

½ cup seasoned dry bread
 crumbs
1 teaspoon grated fresh lemon
 peel
1 teaspoon dried dill weed
1 teaspoon paprika
3 tablespoons all-purpose flour
2 egg whites

1 tablespoon water
1½ pounds Boston scrod or
 orange roughy fillets, cut
 into 6 (4-ounce) pieces
2 tablespoons margarine,
 melted
Tartar Sauce (page 46)
Lemon wedges

1 Preheat oven to 400°F. Spray 15×10-inch jelly-roll pan with nonstick cooking spray. Combine bread crumbs, lemon peel, dill and paprika in shallow bowl or pie plate. Place flour in resealable plastic food storage bag. Beat egg whites and water together in another shallow bowl or pie plate.

2 Add fish, one fillet at a time, to bag. Seal bag; turn to coat fish lightly. Dip fish into egg white mixture, letting excess drip off. Roll fish in bread crumb mixture. Place in prepared jelly-roll pan. Repeat with remaining fish fillets. Brush margarine evenly over fish. Bake 15 to 18 minutes or until fish begins to flake when tested with fork.

3 Prepare Tartar Sauce while fish is baking. Serve fish with lemon wedges and Tartar Sauce. *Makes 6 servings*

continued on page 46

Oven-Roasted Boston Scrod, continued

TARTAR SAUCE

½ cup nonfat or reduced-fat
   mayonnaise
¼ cup sweet pickle relish

2 teaspoons Dijon mustard
¼ teaspoon hot pepper sauce
   (optional)

 Combine all ingredients in small bowl; mix well.   *Makes ⅔ cup*

Nutrients per Serving:

Calories	215 (21% calories from fat)				
Total Fat	5 g	Carbohydrate	18 g	Iron	1 mg
Saturated Fat	1 g	Dietary Fiber	trace	Vitamin A	81 RE
Cholesterol	49 mg	Protein	23 g	Vitamin C	2 mg
Sodium	754 mg	Calcium	31 mg	Sugar	trace

DIETARY EXCHANGES: 1 Starch/Bread, 2½ Lean Meat

Health Note
Scrod and cod are naturally low in fat and calories and
high in valuable omega-3 fatty acids.

SHRIMP ÉTOUFFÉE

The classic Cajun comfort food, étouffée literally means "to smother." This version eliminates most of the fat, but still "smothers" your tastebuds with abundant flavor and spice.

3 tablespoons vegetable oil
¼ cup all-purpose flour
1 cup chopped onion
1 cup chopped green bell
    pepper
½ cup chopped carrots
½ cup chopped celery
4 cloves garlic, minced
1 can (about 14 ounces) clear
    vegetable broth

1 bottle (8 ounces) clam juice
½ teaspoon salt
2½ pounds large shrimp, peeled
    and deveined
1 teaspoon crushed red pepper
1 teaspoon hot pepper sauce
4 cups hot cooked white or
    basmati rice
½ cup chopped flat leaf parsley

1 Heat oil in Dutch oven over medium heat. Add flour; cook and stir 10 to 15 minutes or until flour mixture is deep golden brown. Add onion, bell pepper, carrots, celery and garlic; cook and stir 5 minutes.

2 Stir in vegetable broth, clam juice and salt; bring to a boil. Simmer, uncovered, 10 minutes or until vegetables are tender. Stir in shrimp, red pepper and pepper sauce; simmer 6 to 8 minutes or until shrimp are opaque.

3 Ladle into eight shallow bowls; top each with ½ cup rice. Sprinkle with parsley. Serve with additional pepper sauce, if desired.

Makes 8 servings

Nutrients per Serving:

Calories	306 (20% calories from fat)				
Total Fat	7 g	Carbohydrate	32 g	Iron	5 mg
Saturated Fat	1 g	Dietary Fiber	1 g	Vitamin A	401 RE
Cholesterol	219 mg	Protein	27 g	Vitamin C	36 mg
Sodium	454 mg	Calcium	72 mg	Sugar	2 g

DIETARY EXCHANGES: 1½ Starch/Bread, 3 Lean Meat, 1 Vegetable

HOPPIN' JOHN SUPPER

The traditional good luck New Year's Day feast in the South, hoppin' John is brimming with flavor and perfect for holiday festivities.

1 cup uncooked converted white rice
1 can (about 14 ounces) fat-free reduced-sodium chicken broth
¼ cup water
1 package (16 ounces) frozen black-eyed peas, thawed
1 tablespoon vegetable oil
1 cup chopped onion
1 cup diced carrots
¾ cup thinly sliced celery with tops
3 cloves garlic, minced
12 ounces reduced-sodium lean fully cooked ham, cut into ¾-inch pieces
¾ teaspoon hot pepper sauce
½ teaspoon salt

1 Combine rice, chicken broth and water in large saucepan; bring to a boil over high heat. Reduce heat; cover and simmer 10 minutes. Stir in black-eyed peas; cover and simmer 10 minutes or until rice and peas are tender and liquid is absorbed.

2 Meanwhile, heat oil in large skillet over medium heat. Add onion, carrots, celery and garlic; cook and stir 15 minutes or until vegetables are tender. Add ham; heat through. Add hot rice mixture, pepper sauce and salt; mix well. Cover; cook over low heat 10 minutes. Sprinkle with parsley and serve with additional pepper sauce, if desired.

Makes 8 servings

Nutrients per Serving:

Calories	245 (13% calories from fat)					
Total Fat	3 g	Carbohydrate	38 g	Iron	3 mg
Saturated Fat	1 g	Dietary Fiber	4 g	Vitamin A	393 RE
Cholesterol	20 mg	Protein	16 g	Vitamin C	6 mg
Sodium	624 mg	Calcium	42 mg	Sugar	3 g

DIETARY EXCHANGES: 2 Starch/Bread, 1 Lean Meat, 1½ Vegetable

MUSTARD-CRUSTED ROAST PORK

3 tablespoons Dijon mustard
4 teaspoons minced garlic,
    divided
2 whole well-trimmed pork
    tenderloins, about
    1 pound each
2 tablespoons dried thyme
1 teaspoon ground black pepper
½ teaspoon salt

1 pound asparagus spears, ends
    trimmed
2 red or yellow bell peppers (or
    one of each), cut lengthwise
    into ½-inch-wide strips
1 cup fat-free reduced-sodium
    chicken broth, divided

1 Preheat oven to 375°F. Combine mustard and 3 teaspoons garlic in small bowl. Spread mustard mixture evenly over top and sides of both tenderloins. Combine thyme, black pepper and salt in small bowl; reserve 1 teaspoon mixture. Sprinkle remaining mixture evenly over tenderloins, patting so that seasoning adheres to mustard. Place tenderloins on rack in shallow roasting pan. Roast 25 minutes.

2 Arrange asparagus and bell peppers in single layer in shallow casserole or 13×9-inch baking pan. Add ¼ cup broth, reserved thyme mixture and remaining 1 teaspoon garlic; toss to coat.

3 Roast vegetables in oven alongside tenderloins 15 to 20 minutes or until thermometer inserted into center of pork registers 160°F and vegetables are tender. Transfer tenderloins to carving board; tent with foil and let stand 5 minutes. Arrange vegetables on serving platter, reserving juices in dish; cover and keep warm. Add remaining ¾ cup broth and juices in dish to roasting pan. Place over range top burner(s); simmer 3 to 4 minutes over medium-high heat or until juices are reduced to ¾ cup, stirring frequently. Carve tenderloins crosswise into ¼-inch slices; arrange on serving platter. Spoon juices over pork and vegetables.

Makes 8 servings

Nutrients per Serving:

Calories	182 (23% calories from fat)				
Total Fat	5 g	Carbohydrate	8 g	Iron	4 mg
Saturated Fat	2 g	Dietary Fiber	1 g	Vitamin A	392 RE
Cholesterol	65 mg	Protein	27 g	Vitamin C	134 mg
Sodium	304 mg	Calcium	55 mg	Sugar	trace

DIETARY EXCHANGES: 3 Lean Meat, 1 Vegetable

HAZELNUT-COATED SALMON STEAKS

In the United States, hazelnuts (also called filberts) are grown almost exclusively in Oregon, and a single tree will yield nuts for hundreds of years. The skins are bitter, so it is best to remove them.

¼ cup hazelnuts
4 salmon steaks, about 5 ounces
   each
1 tablespoon apple butter

1 tablespoon Dijon mustard
¼ teaspoon dried thyme leaves
⅛ teaspoon ground black pepper
2 cups cooked white rice

1 Preheat oven to 375°F. Place hazelnuts on baking sheet; bake 8 minutes or until lightly browned. Quickly transfer nuts to clean dry dish towel. Fold towel; rub vigorously to remove as much of the skins as possible. Finely chop hazelnuts using food processor, nut grinder or chef's knife.

2 *Increase oven temperature to 450°F.* Place salmon in baking dish. Combine apple butter, mustard, thyme and pepper in small bowl. Brush on salmon; top each steak with nuts. Bake 14 to 16 minutes or until salmon flakes easily with fork. Serve with rice and steamed snow peas, if desired.

Makes 4 servings

Nutrients per Serving:

Calories	329 (30% calories from fat)				
Total Fat	11 g	Carbohydrate	26 g	Iron	3 mg
Saturated Fat	1 g	Dietary Fiber	1 g	Vitamin A	45 RE
Cholesterol	72 mg	Protein	31 g	Vitamin C	trace
Sodium	143 mg	Calcium	34 mg	Sugar	trace

DIETARY EXCHANGES: 1½ Starch/Bread, 4 Lean Meat

Health Note

Salmon is one of the richest sources of omega-3 fatty acids. Evidence suggests that these acids may prevent blood clots, lessen arthritis pain and help treat the skin disorder psoriasis.

EASY BRUNCH FRITTATA

*This Italian omelet is an ideal alternative to quiche
for your next brunch.*

1 cup small broccoli flowerets
2½ cups (12 ounces) frozen hash
    brown potatoes with onions
    and peppers (O'Brien style),
    thawed
1½ cups cholesterol-free egg
    substitute, thawed

2 tablespoons 2% low-fat milk
¾ teaspoon salt
¼ teaspoon ground black pepper
½ cup (2 ounces) shredded
    reduced-fat Cheddar cheese

1 Preheat oven to 450°F. Coat medium nonstick ovenproof skillet with nonstick cooking spray. Heat skillet over medium heat until hot. Add broccoli; cook and stir 2 minutes. Add potatoes; cook and stir 5 minutes.

2 Beat together egg substitute, milk, salt and pepper in small bowl; pour over potato mixture. Cook 5 minutes or until edges are set (center will still be wet).

3 Transfer skillet to oven; bake 6 minutes or until center is set. Sprinkle with cheese; let stand 2 to 3 minutes or until cheese is melted.

4 Cut into wedges; serve with low-fat sour cream, if desired.

Makes 6 servings

Nutrients per Serving:

Calories	102 (20% calories from fat)				
Total Fat	2 g	Carbohydrate	11 g	Iron	2 mg
Saturated Fat	1 g	Dietary Fiber	1 g	Vitamin A	135 RE
Cholesterol	7 mg	Protein	9 g	Vitamin C	23 mg
Sodium	627 mg	Calcium	124 mg	Sugar	1 g

DIETARY EXCHANGES: ½ Starch/Bread, 1 Lean Meat

SIDE DISHES

SOUTHERN-STYLE SUCCOTASH

Taken from the Indian word meaning "boiled whole kernels of corn," succotash is a true favorite of the South. Hominy, corn kernels that have had their germ and hulls removed, is readily available in most supermarkets; it is high in calcium and B vitamins.

2 tablespoons margarine
1 cup chopped onion
1 package (10 ounces) frozen lima beans, thawed
1 cup frozen whole corn kernels, thawed
½ cup chopped red bell pepper
1 can (15 to 16 ounces) hominy, drained

⅓ cup fat-free reduced-sodium chicken broth
½ teaspoon salt
¼ teaspoon hot pepper sauce
¼ cup chopped green onion tops or chives

1 Melt margarine in large nonstick skillet over medium heat. Add onion; cook and stir 5 minutes. Add lima beans, corn and bell pepper. Cook and stir 5 minutes.

2 Add hominy, chicken broth, salt and pepper sauce; simmer 5 minutes or until most of liquid has evaporated. Remove from heat; stir in green onions. Serve with Festive Cornmeal Biscuits (page 68), if desired.

Makes 6 servings

Nutrients per Serving:

Calories	175 (23% calories from fat)				
Total Fat	5 g	Carbohydrate	29 g	Iron	2 mg
Saturated Fat	1 g	Dietary Fiber	5 g	Vitamin A	197 RE
Cholesterol	0 mg	Protein	6 g	Vitamin C	48 mg
Sodium	406 mg	Calcium	33 mg	Sugar	3 g

DIETARY EXCHANGES: 2 Starch/Bread, 1 Fat

SPIRITED SWEET POTATO CASSEROLE

Sweet potatoes were introduced to the South by Africans and have become synonymous with "Southern cooking." High in vitamins C and A, sweet potatoes are available year-round.

2½ pounds sweet potatoes
2 tablespoons reduced-calorie margarine
⅓ cup 1% low-fat or skim milk
¼ cup packed brown sugar
2 tablespoons bourbon or apple juice

1 teaspoon ground cinnamon
1 teaspoon vanilla
2 egg whites
½ teaspoon salt
⅓ cup chopped pecans

1 Preheat oven to 375°F. Bake potatoes 50 to 60 minutes or until very tender. Cool 10 minutes; leave oven on. Scoop pulp from warm potatoes into large bowl; discard potato skins. Add margarine to bowl; mash with potato masher until potatoes are fairly smooth and margarine has melted. Stir in milk, brown sugar, bourbon, cinnamon and vanilla; mix well.

2 Beat egg whites with electric mixer at high speed until soft peaks form. Add salt; beat until stiff peaks form. Fold egg whites into sweet potato mixture.

3 Spray 1½-quart soufflé dish with nonstick cooking spray. Spoon sweet potato mixture into dish; top with pecans.

4 Bake 30 to 35 minutes or until casserole is puffed and pecans are toasted. Serve immediately.

Makes 8 servings

Nutrients per Serving:

Calories	203 (21% calories from fat)					
Total Fat	5 g	Carbohydrate	35 g	Iron	1 mg
Saturated Fat	1 g	Dietary Fiber	trace	Vitamin A	1923 RE
Cholesterol	trace	Protein	3 g	Vitamin C	19 mg
Sodium	202 mg	Calcium	48 mg	Sugar	1 g

DIETARY EXCHANGES: 2 Starch/Bread, 1½ Fat

POTATO PANCAKES WITH APPLE-CHERRY CHUTNEY

Apple-Cherry Chutney (recipe follows)
1 pound baking potatoes, about 2 medium
½ small onion
3 egg whites

2 tablespoons all-purpose flour
½ teaspoon salt
¼ teaspoon ground black pepper
4 teaspoons vegetable oil, divided

1 Prepare Apple-Cherry Chutney; set aside.

2 Peel potatoes; cut into chunks. Combine potatoes, onion, egg whites, flour, salt and pepper in food processor or blender; process until almost smooth (mixture will appear grainy).

3 Heat large nonstick skillet 1 minute over medium heat. Add 1 teaspoon oil. Spoon 2 tablespoons batter per pancake into skillet. Cook 3 pancakes at a time, 3 minutes per side or until golden brown. Repeat with remaining batter, adding 1 teaspoon oil with each batch. Serve with Apple-Cherry Chutney.

Makes 1 dozen pancakes (2 pancakes per serving)

APPLE–CHERRY CHUTNEY

1 cup chunky applesauce
½ cup canned tart cherries, drained
2 tablespoons brown sugar

1 teaspoon lemon juice
½ teaspoon ground cinnamon
⅛ teaspoon ground nutmeg

1 Combine all ingredients in small saucepan; bring to a boil. Reduce heat; simmer 5 minutes. Serve warm.

Makes 1½ cups

Nutrients per Serving:

Calories	164 (17% calories from fat)				
Total Fat	3 g	Carbohydrate	31 g	Iron	1 mg
Saturated Fat	trace	Dietary Fiber	1 g	Vitamin A	17 RE
Cholesterol	0 mg	Protein	4 g	Vitamin C	12 mg
Sodium	214 mg	Calcium	18 mg	Sugar	2 g

DIETARY EXCHANGES: 1½ Starch/Bread, ½ Fruit, ½ Fat

WILD & BROWN RICE WITH EXOTIC MUSHROOMS

1⅔ cups packaged unseasoned
    wild & brown rice blend
 6 cups water
½ ounce dried porcini or morel
    mushrooms
¾ cup boiling water
 2 tablespoons margarine
 8 ounces cremini (brown) or
    button mushrooms, sliced

2 cloves garlic, minced
2 tablespoons chopped fresh
    thyme *or* 2 teaspoons dried
    thyme leaves
1 teaspoon salt
¼ teaspoon ground black pepper
½ cup sliced green onions

1 Combine rice and water in large saucepan; bring to a boil over high heat. Cover; simmer over low heat until rice is tender (check package for cooking time). Drain, but do not rinse.*

2 Meanwhile, combine porcini mushrooms and boiling water in small bowl; let stand 30 minutes or until mushrooms are tender. Drain mushrooms, reserving liquid. Chop mushrooms; set aside.

3 Melt margarine in large, deep skillet over medium heat. Add cremini mushrooms and garlic; cook and stir 5 minutes. Sprinkle thyme, salt and pepper over mushrooms; cook and stir 1 minute or until mushrooms are tender.

4 Stir drained rice, porcini mushrooms and reserved mushroom liquid into skillet; cook and stir over medium-low heat 5 minutes or until hot. Stir in green onions. *Makes 8 servings*

*Rice may be prepared up to 3 hours before serving and kept covered at room temperature until it is added to fresh mushroom mixture.

Nutrients per Serving:

Calories	175 (21% calories from fat)				
Total Fat	4 g	Carbohydrate	30 g	Iron	1 mg
Saturated Fat	1 g	Dietary Fiber	2 g	Vitamin A	61 RE
Cholesterol	0 mg	Protein	5 g	Vitamin C	1 mg
Sodium	304 mg	Calcium	23 mg	Sugar	1 g

DIETARY EXCHANGES: 2 Starch/Bread, 1 Fat

SPICY SOUTHWESTERN VEGETABLE SAUTÉ

The staples of Southwestern cuisine are featured in this mélange of spice and savor. Adding more jalapeño peppers will certainly indulge those with a "fiery" palate.

1 bag (16 ounces) frozen green beans
2 tablespoons water
1 tablespoon olive oil
1 red bell pepper, chopped
1 medium yellow summer squash or zucchini, chopped
1 jalapeño pepper, seeded, chopped*

½ teaspoon garlic powder
½ teaspoon ground cumin
½ teaspoon chili powder
¼ cup sliced green onions
2 tablespoons chopped fresh cilantro (optional)
1 tablespoon brown sugar

1 Heat large skillet over medium heat; add green beans, water and oil. Cover; cook 4 minutes, stirring occasionally.

2 Add bell pepper, squash, jalapeño, garlic powder, cumin and chili powder. Cook uncovered, stirring occasionally, 4 minutes or until vegetables are crisp-tender. Stir in green onions, cilantro, if desired, and brown sugar.

Makes 6 servings

*Jalapeños can sting and irritate the skin; wear rubber gloves when handling peppers and do not touch eyes. Wash hands after handling.

Nutrients per Serving:

Calories	67 (30% calories from fat)				
Total Fat	3 g	Carbohydrate	11 g	Iron	1 mg
Saturated Fat	trace	Dietary Fiber	2 g	Vitamin A	292 RE
Cholesterol	0 mg	Protein	2 g	Vitamin C	91 mg
Sodium	110 mg	Calcium	40 mg	Sugar	trace

DIETARY EXCHANGES: 2 Vegetable, ½ Fat

FESTIVE CORNMEAL BISCUITS

Another Southern favorite, these biscuits eliminate butter and cream and result in a low-fat treat brimming with heavenly goodness.

1¾ cups all-purpose flour
½ cup yellow cornmeal
1 tablespoon baking powder
1 tablespoon sugar
1 teaspoon salt
¼ teaspoon baking soda

3 tablespoons margarine
¾ cup buttermilk
1 egg white, beaten
Peach or strawberry preserves (optional)

1 Preheat oven to 425°F. Combine flour, cornmeal, baking powder, sugar, salt and baking soda in large bowl; mix well. Cut in margarine with pastry blender or two knives until mixture forms coarse crumbs. Add buttermilk; mix just until dough holds together.

2 Turn dough out onto lightly floured surface; knead 8 to 10 times. Pat dough to ½-inch thickness; cut with decorative 2-inch cookie or biscuit cutter. Spray baking sheet with nonstick cooking spray and place biscuits on sheet. Brush tops lightly with beaten egg white.

3 Bake 12 to 13 minutes or until light golden brown. Serve with preserves, if desired.   *Makes 1 dozen biscuits (1 biscuit per serving)*

Nutrients per Serving:

Calories	122 (25% calories from fat)					
Total Fat	3 g	Carbohydrate	20 g	Iron	1 mg
Saturated Fat	1 g	Dietary Fiber	1 g	Vitamin A	39 RE
Cholesterol	1 mg	Protein	3 g	Vitamin C	trace
Sodium	341 mg	Calcium	38 mg	Sugar	2 g

DIETARY EXCHANGES: 1½ Starch/Bread, ½ Fat

CARROT AND PARSNIP PURÉE

*This simple-to-prepare creation takes ordinary veggies
and transforms them into a creamy delight low in fat but high
in satisfaction. The enticing color will add sparkle to any
holiday table.*

1 pound carrots, peeled
1 pound parsnips, peeled
1 cup chopped onion

1 cup clear vegetable broth
1 tablespoon margarine
⅛ teaspoon ground nutmeg

1 Cut carrots and parsnips crosswise into ½-inch pieces.

2 Combine carrots, parsnips, onion and vegetable broth in medium saucepan. Cover; bring to a boil over high heat. Reduce heat; simmer, covered, 20 to 22 minutes or until vegetables are very tender.

3 Drain vegetables, reserving broth. Combine vegetables, margarine, nutmeg and ¼ cup reserved broth in food processor. Process until smooth. Serve immediately.

Makes 10 servings

Nutrients per Serving:

Calories	78 (15% calories from fat)					
Total Fat	1 g	Carbohydrate	16 g	Iron	1 mg
Saturated Fat	trace	Dietary Fiber	3 g	Vitamin A	1137 RE
Cholesterol	0 mg	Protein	1 g	Vitamin C	8 mg
Sodium	56 mg	Calcium	35 mg	Sugar	trace

DIETARY EXCHANGES: 3 Vegetable

Cook's Tip

If you want to prepare this dish ahead of time, transfer
the completed purée to a microwavable casserole
and chill up to 24 hours. To reheat, microwave
covered at HIGH 6 to 7 minutes, stirring after
4 minutes of cooking.

Desserts

CARAMELIZED PEACHES & CREAM

Divine and dazzling are only two ways to describe this down-home Southern delight. It's a satisfying finale to any holiday feast.

2 pounds (about 8 medium)
 sliced peeled peaches, or
 thawed and well-drained
 unsweetened frozen peaches
2 tablespoons bourbon
¾ cup reduced-fat sour cream

½ teaspoon ground cinnamon
¼ teaspoon ground nutmeg
¾ cup packed light brown sugar
8 slices (1½ ounces each) angel
 food cake, cut into cubes

1 Toss peaches with bourbon in shallow ovenproof 1½-quart casserole or 11×7-inch glass baking dish. Press down into even layer.

2 Combine sour cream, cinnamon and nutmeg in small bowl; mix well. Spoon mixture evenly over peaches. (Mixture may be covered and refrigerated up to 2 hours before cooking time.)

3 Preheat broiler. Sprinkle brown sugar evenly over sour cream mixture to cover. Broil 4 to 5 inches from heat, 3 to 5 minutes or until brown sugar is melted and bubbly. (Watch closely after 3 minutes so that sugar does not burn.)

4 Spoon immediately over angel food cake.   *Makes 10 servings*

Nutrients per Serving:

Calories	215 (6% calories from fat)				
Total Fat	1 g	Carbohydrate	47 g	Iron	1 mg
Saturated Fat	trace	Dietary Fiber	1 g	Vitamin A	117 RE
Cholesterol	6 mg	Protein	3 g	Vitamin C	6 mg
Sodium	272 mg	Calcium	91 mg	Sugar	8 g

DIETARY EXCHANGES: 2½ Starch/Bread, ½ Fruit

APPLE-CRANBERRY CRESCENT COOKIES

1¼ cups chopped apples
½ cup dried cranberries
½ cup reduced-fat sour cream
¼ cup cholesterol-free egg substitute
¼ cup margarine or butter, melted

3 tablespoons sugar, divided
1 package quick-rise yeast
1 teaspoon vanilla
2 cups all-purpose flour
1 teaspoon ground cinnamon
1 tablespoon reduced-fat (2%) milk

1 Preheat oven to 350°F. Lightly coat cookie sheet with nonstick cooking spray; set aside.

2 Place apples and cranberries in food processor or blender; pulse to finely chop. Set aside.

3 Combine sour cream, egg substitute, margarine and 2 tablespoons sugar in medium bowl. Add yeast and vanilla. Add flour; stir to form ball. Turn dough out onto lightly floured work surface. Knead 1 minute. Cover with plastic wrap; allow to stand 10 minutes.

4 Divide dough into thirds. Roll one portion to 12-inch circle. Spread with ⅓ apple mixture (about ¼ cup). Cut dough to make 8 wedges. Roll up each wedge beginning at outside edge. Place on prepared cookie sheet; turn ends of cookies to form crescents. Repeat with remaining dough and apple mixture.

5 Combine remaining 1 tablespoon sugar and cinnamon in small bowl. Lightly brush cookies with milk; sprinkle with sugar-cinnamon mixture. Bake cookies 18 to 20 minutes or until lightly browned.

Makes 24 servings

Nutrients per Serving:					
Calories	82 (27% calories from fat)				
Total Fat	2 g	Sodium	31 mg	Protein	2 g
Saturated Fat	1 g	Carbohydrate	13 g		
Cholesterol	2 mg	Dietary Fiber	1 g		
DIETARY EXCHANGES: 1 Starch					

THUMBPRINT COOKIES

1½ cups all-purpose flour
1 teaspoon baking soda
¼ teaspoon salt
⅔ cup sugar
¼ cup margarine, softened

1 egg white
1 teaspoon vanilla
½ cup no-sugar-added raspberry
   or apricot fruit spread

1 Combine flour, baking soda and salt in medium bowl; set aside. Beat sugar, margarine, egg white and vanilla in large bowl with electric mixer at high speed until blended. Add flour mixture; mix well. Press mixture together to form a ball. Refrigerate ½ hour or overnight.

2 Preheat oven to 375°F. Lightly coat cookie sheet with nonstick cooking spray; set aside.

3 Shape dough into 1-inch balls with lightly floured hands; place on cookie sheet. Press down with thumb in center of each ball to form indention.

4 Bake 10 to 12 minutes or until golden brown. Remove to wire rack and cool completely. Fill each indention with about 1 teaspoon fruit spread.

Makes about 20 servings

Nutrients per Serving:

Calories	90 (24% calories from fat)					
Total Fat	2 g	Sodium	130 mg	Protein	1 g
Saturated Fat	<1 g	Carbohydrate	16 g		
Cholesterol	0 mg	Dietary Fiber	<1 g		

DIETARY EXCHANGES: 1 Starch, ½ Fat

MAPLE PUMPKIN PIE

Nothing says "holidays" like pumpkin pie. The addition of maple syrup gives it a snappy New England accent.

1⅓ cups all-purpose flour
⅓ cup plus 1 tablespoon sugar, divided
¾ teaspoon salt, divided
2 tablespoons vegetable shortening
2 tablespoons margarine
4 to 5 tablespoons ice water
1 can (15 ounces) solid-pack pumpkin

2 egg whites
1 cup evaporated skimmed milk
⅓ cup maple syrup
1 teaspoon ground cinnamon
½ teaspoon ground ginger
Thawed reduced-fat whipped topping (optional)

1 Combine flour, 1 tablespoon sugar and ¼ teaspoon salt in medium bowl. Cut in shortening and margarine with pastry blender or two knives until mixture forms coarse crumbs. Mix in ice water, 1 tablespoon at a time, until mixture comes together and forms a soft dough. Wrap in plastic wrap. Refrigerate 30 minutes.

2 Preheat oven to 425°F. Roll out pastry on floured surface to ⅛-inch thickness. Cut into 12-inch circle. Ease pastry into 9-inch pie plate; turn edge under and flute edge.

3 Combine pumpkin, remaining ⅓ cup sugar, egg whites, milk, syrup, cinnamon, ginger and remaining ½ teaspoon salt in large bowl; mix well. Pour into unbaked pie shell. Bake 15 minutes; *reduce oven temperature to 350°F.* Continue baking 45 to 50 minutes or until center is set. Transfer to wire cooling rack; let stand at least 30 minutes before serving. Serve warm, at room temperature or chilled with whipped topping, if desired.

Makes 10 servings

Nutrients per Serving:

Calories	198 (22% calories from fat)				
Total Fat	5 g	Carbohydrate	34 g	Iron	2 mg
Saturated Fat	1 g	Dietary Fiber	2 g	Vitamin A	996 RE
Cholesterol	1 mg	Protein	5 g	Vitamin C	2 mg
Sodium	231 mg	Calcium	103 mg	Sugar	14 g

DIETARY EXCHANGES: 2 Starch/Bread, 1 Fat

TROPICAL FRUIT CREAM PARFAITS

*Chock-full of vitamins A, C and D, mangoes are an exotic change
of pace from more commonplace fruits. Tortilla sticks
provide a Southwestern twist.*

1 cup 2% low-fat milk
1 package (4-serving size)
   sugar-free vanilla instant
   pudding mix

½ cup mango nectar
Cinnamon-Ginger Tortilla
   Sticks (recipe follows)
1 large orange, peeled, chopped

1 Pour milk into medium bowl. Add pudding mix; stir with wire whisk 1
minute or until smooth and thickened. Stir in mango nectar; chill.

2 Prepare Cinnamon-Ginger Tortilla Sticks. Reserve 10 sticks; divide
remaining sticks equally in 5 parfait dishes or small glasses. Top each
with pudding mixture, orange and two reserved tortilla sticks.

Makes 5 servings

CINNAMON–GINGER TORTILLA STICKS

3 tablespoons brown sugar
2 tablespoons margarine
½ teaspoon ground ginger

½ teaspoon ground cinnamon
4 (6-inch) flour tortillas, cut
   into ½-inch strips

1 Preheat oven to 375°F. Combine sugar, margarine, ginger and
cinnamon in small microwavable bowl. Microwave at HIGH 1 minute or
until smooth when stirred.

2 Twist tortillas into spirals and arrange on baking sheet sprayed with
nonstick cooking spray. Brush each with brown sugar mixture. Bake 10 to
12 minutes or until edges are lightly browned; cool.

Makes 5 servings

Nutrients per Serving:

Calories	277 (22% calories from fat)				
Total Fat	7 g	Carbohydrate	51 g	Iron	trace
Saturated Fat	4 g	Dietary Fiber	1 g	Vitamin A	84 RE
Cholesterol	16 mg	Protein	4 g	Vitamin C	16 mg
Sodium	357 mg	Calcium	85 mg	Sugar	5 g

DIETARY EXCHANGES: ½ Milk, 3 Fruit, 1 Fat

COCOA HAZELNUT MACAROONS

To satisfy your holiday sweet tooth without cheating on your diet, bake up a batch of these moist and chewy cookies. Hazelnuts add just the right amount of delicate nuttiness to these tantalizing morsels.

⅓ cup hazelnuts
¾ cup quick oats
⅓ cup packed brown sugar
6 tablespoons unsweetened cocoa powder
2 tablespoons all-purpose flour

4 egg whites
1 teaspoon vanilla
½ teaspoon salt
⅓ cup plus 1 tablespoon granulated sugar

1 Preheat oven to 375°F. Place hazelnuts on baking sheet; bake 8 minutes or until lightly browned. Quickly transfer nuts to dry dish towel. Fold towel; rub vigorously to remove as much of the skins as possible. Finely chop hazelnuts using food processor, nut grinder or chef's knife. Combine with oats, brown sugar, cocoa and flour in medium bowl; mix well. Set aside.

2 *Reduce oven temperature to 325°F.* Combine egg whites, vanilla and salt in clean dry medium mixing bowl. Beat with electric mixer on high until soft peaks form. Gradually add granulated sugar, continuing to beat on high until stiff peaks form. Gently fold in hazelnut mixture with rubber spatula.

3 Drop level measuring tablespoonfuls of dough onto cookie sheet. Bake 15 to 17 minutes or until tops of cookies no longer appear wet. Transfer to cooling rack. Store in loosely covered container.

Makes 3 dozen cookies (3 cookies per serving)

Nutrients per Serving:

Calories	104 (24% calories from fat)				
Total Fat	3 g	Carbohydrate	18 g	Iron	1 mg
Saturated Fat	trace	Dietary Fiber	1 g	Vitamin A	trace
Cholesterol	0 mg	Protein	3 g	Vitamin C	trace
Sodium	112 mg	Calcium	22 mg	Sugar	6 g

DIETARY EXCHANGES: 1 Starch/Bread, ½ Fat

MAPLE CARAMEL BREAD PUDDING

Could bread pudding this creamy and melt-in-your-mouth delicious be low in fat and so easy to prepare? Absolutely!

8 slices cinnamon raisin bread
2 whole eggs
1 egg white
⅓ cup sugar
1½ cups 2% low-fat milk
½ cup maple syrup

½ teaspoon cinnamon
¼ teaspoon ground nutmeg
¼ teaspoon salt
6 tablespoons fat-free caramel
    ice cream topping

1 Preheat oven to 350°F. Spray 8×8-inch baking dish with nonstick cooking spray. Cut bread into ¾-inch cubes; arrange in prepared dish.

2 Beat whole eggs, egg white and sugar in medium bowl. Beat in milk, syrup, cinnamon, nutmeg and salt; pour evenly over bread. Toss bread gently to coat.

3 Bake 45 minutes or until center is set. Transfer dish to wire cooling rack; let stand 20 minutes before serving. Serve warm with caramel topping.

Makes 8 servings

Nutrients per Serving:

Calories	235 (12% calories from fat)				
Total Fat	3 g	Carbohydrate	47 g	Iron	1 mg
Saturated Fat	1 g	Dietary Fiber	trace	Vitamin A	52 RE
Cholesterol	57 mg	Protein	6 g	Vitamin C	trace
Sodium	228 mg	Calcium	109 mg	Sugar	31 g

DIETARY EXCHANGES: 3 Starch/Bread, ½ Fat

MOCHA CRINKLES

1¾ cups all-purpose flour
¾ cup unsweetened cocoa
   powder
2 teaspoons instant espresso or
   coffee granules
1 teaspoon baking soda
¼ teaspoon salt

⅛ teaspoon ground black pepper
1⅓ cups packed light brown sugar
½ cup vegetable oil
¼ cup low-fat sour cream
1 egg
1 teaspoon vanilla
½ cup powdered sugar

1 Mix flour, cocoa, espresso, baking soda, salt and pepper in medium bowl; set aside.

2 Beat brown sugar and oil in another medium bowl with electric mixer at medium speed until well blended. Beat in sour cream, egg and vanilla.

3 Beat in flour mixture until soft dough forms. Form dough into disc; cover. Refrigerate dough until firm, 3 to 4 hours.

4 Preheat oven to 350°F. Place powdered sugar in shallow bowl. Cut dough into 1-inch pieces; roll into balls. Coat with powdered sugar. Place on ungreased cookie sheets.

5 Bake 10 to 12 minutes or until tops of cookies are firm to the touch. *Do not overbake.* Cool cookies completely on wire racks.

Makes 6 dozen cookies (1 cookie per serving)

Nutrients per Serving:

Calories	44 (30% calories from fat)				
Total Fat	1 g	Carbohydrate	7 g	Iron	1 mg
Saturated Fat	trace	Dietary Fiber	0 g	Vitamin A	4 RE
Cholesterol	3 mg	Protein	0 g	Vitamin C	0 mg
Sodium	28 mg	Calcium	7 mg	Sugar	trace

DIETARY EXCHANGES: ½ Starch/Bread

TURTLE CHEESECAKE

6 tablespoons reduced-calorie margarine
1½ cups graham cracker crumbs
2 envelopes unflavored gelatin
2 packages (8 ounces each) fat-free cream cheese
2 cups 1% low-fat cottage cheese
1 cup sugar

1½ teaspoons vanilla
1 container (8 ounces) thawed reduced-fat nondairy whipped topping
¼ cup prepared fat-free caramel topping
¼ cup prepared fat-free hot fudge topping
¼ cup chopped pecans

1 Preheat oven to 350°F. Spray bottom and side of 9-inch springform pan with nonstick cooking spray. Melt margarine in small saucepan over medium heat. Stir in graham cracker crumbs. Press crumb mixture firmly onto bottom and side of prepared pan. Bake 10 minutes. Cool.

2 Place ½ cup cold water in small saucepan; sprinkle gelatin over water. Let stand 3 minutes to soften. Heat gelatin mixture over low heat until completely dissolved, stirring constantly.

3 Combine cream cheese, cottage cheese, sugar and vanilla in food processor or blender; process until smooth. Add gelatin mixture; process until well blended. Fold in whipped topping. Pour into prepared crust. Refrigerate 4 hours or until set.

4 Loosen cake from side of pan. Remove side of pan from cake. Drizzle caramel and hot fudge toppings over cake. Sprinkle pecans evenly over top of cake before serving. *Makes 16 servings*

Nutrients per Serving:

Calories	231 (26% calories from fat)				
Total Fat	7 g	Carbohydrate	33 g	Iron	1 mg
Saturated Fat	3 g	Dietary Fiber	trace	Vitamin A	151 RE
Cholesterol	1 mg	Protein	9 g	Vitamin C	1 mg
Sodium	419 mg	Calcium	127 mg	Sugar	18 g

DIETARY EXCHANGES: 2 Starch/Bread, ½ Lean Meat, 1 Fat

APPLE-CRANBERRY TART

Excellent baking apples such as Jonathan, Jonagold or Rome Beauty are at their peak during the winter months.

Tart Dough (page 92)
⅓ cup dried cranberries
½ cup boiling water
¾ cup sugar
 1 teaspoon ground cinnamon

2 tablespoons cornstarch
4 medium baking apples
 Vanilla frozen yogurt
 (optional)

1 Prepare Tart Dough.

2 Preheat oven to 425°F. Combine cranberries and boiling water in small bowl. Let stand 20 minutes or until softened.

3 Roll out Tart Dough on floured surface to ⅛-inch thickness. Cut into 11-inch circle. If leftover dough remains, use scraps for decorating top of tart. Ease dough into 10-inch tart pan with removable bottom, leaving ¼ inch of dough above rim of pan. Prick bottom and sides of dough with tines of fork; bake 12 minutes or until dough begins to brown. Cool on wire rack. *Reduce oven temperature to 375°F.*

4 Combine ¾ cup sugar and cinnamon in large bowl; mix well. Reserve 1 teaspoon mixture for sprinkling over top of tart. Add cornstarch to bowl; mix well. Peel, core and thinly slice apples, adding pieces to bowl as they are sliced; toss well. Drain cranberries. Add to apple mixture; toss well.

5 Arrange apple mixture attractively over dough. Sprinkle reserved 1 teaspoon sugar mixture evenly over top of tart. Place tart on baking sheet; bake 30 to 35 minutes or until apples are tender and crust is golden brown. Cool on wire rack. Remove side of pan; place tart on serving plate. Serve warm or at room temperature with frozen yogurt, if desired.

Makes 8 servings

continued on page 92

Apple-Cranberry Tart, continued

TART DOUGH

1⅓ cups all-purpose flour
1 tablespoon sugar
¼ teaspoon salt
2 tablespoons vegetable
   shortening

2 tablespoons margarine
4 to 5 tablespoons ice water

1 Combine flour, sugar and salt in medium bowl. Cut in shortening and margarine with pastry blender or two knives until mixture forms coarse crumbs. Mix in ice water, 1 tablespoon at a time, until mixture comes together and forms a soft dough. Wrap in plastic wrap. Refrigerate 30 minutes.

Nutrients per Serving:

Calories	263 (22% calories from fat)				
Total Fat	6 g	Carbohydrate	50 g	Iron	1 mg
Saturated Fat	2 g	Dietary Fiber	2 g	Vitamin A	4 RE
Cholesterol	0 mg	Protein	2 g	Vitamin C	5 mg
Sodium	68 mg	Calcium	13 mg	Sugar	29 g

DIETARY EXCHANGES: 1½ Starch/Bread, 1½ Fruit, 1½ Fat

Cook's Tip
The dough can be made in a food processor, but a little care must be taken to avoid a tough crust. Combine the dry ingredients using a few on/off pulses. Add small chunks of cold margarine and use a few more on/off pulses until the mixture resembles small marbles. Add the ice water, again using a few on/off pulses, just until the dough starts to gather on the blade. Turn the mixture out onto a piece of plastic wrap and form the dough into a disk. Refrigerate.

METRIC CONVERSION CHART

VOLUME MEASUREMENTS (dry)

$^1/_8$ teaspoon = 0.5 mL
$^1/_4$ teaspoon = 1 mL
$^1/_2$ teaspoon = 2 mL
$^3/_4$ teaspoon = 4 mL
1 teaspoon = 5 mL
1 tablespoon = 15 mL
2 tablespoons = 30 mL
$^1/_4$ cup = 60 mL
$^1/_3$ cup = 75 mL
$^1/_2$ cup = 125 mL
$^2/_3$ cup = 150 mL
$^3/_4$ cup = 175 mL
1 cup = 250 mL
2 cups = 1 pint = 500 mL
3 cups = 750 mL
4 cups = 1 quart = 1 L

VOLUME MEASUREMENTS (fluid)

1 fluid ounce (2 tablespoons) = 30 mL
4 fluid ounces ($^1/_2$ cup) = 125 mL
8 fluid ounces (1 cup) = 250 mL
12 fluid ounces (1$^1/_2$ cups) = 375 mL
16 fluid ounces (2 cups) = 500 mL

WEIGHTS (mass)

$^1/_2$ ounce = 15 g
1 ounce = 30 g
3 ounces = 90 g
4 ounces = 120 g
8 ounces = 225 g
10 ounces = 285 g
12 ounces = 360 g
16 ounces = 1 pound = 450 g

DIMENSIONS

$^1/_{16}$ inch = 2 mm
$^1/_8$ inch = 3 mm
$^1/_4$ inch = 6 mm
$^1/_2$ inch = 1.5 cm
$^3/_4$ inch = 2 cm
1 inch = 2.5 cm

OVEN TEMPERATURES

250°F = 120°C
275°F = 140°C
300°F = 150°C
325°F = 160°C
350°F = 180°C
375°F = 190°C
400°F = 200°C
425°F = 220°C
450°F = 230°C

BAKING PAN SIZES

Utensil	Size in Inches/Quarts	Metric Volume	Size in Centimeters
Baking or Cake Pan (square or rectangular)	8×8×2	2 L	20×20×5
	9×9×2	2.5 L	23×23×5
	12×8×2	3 L	30×20×5
	13×9×2	3.5 L	33×23×5
Loaf Pan	8×4×3	1.5 L	20×10×7
	9×5×3	2 L	23×13×7
Round Layer Cake Pan	8×1½	1.2 L	20×4
	9×1½	1.5 L	23×4
Pie Plate	8×1¼	750 mL	20×3
	9×1¼	1 L	23×3
Baking Dish or Casserole	1 quart	1 L	—
	1½ quart	1.5 L	—
	2 quart	2 L	—